Treading Water

Synclaire A. Warren

Treading Water

Cover art by Angela Lofton-Moore of Info Princess

Published in the United States of America

Sunshine Solutions Publishing
9912 Business Park Drive, Ste. 170
Sacramento, CA 95827

Library of Congress Control Number   2018945862

ISBN-13: 978-1719445030
ISBN-10: 1719445036

  1) Poetry
  2) Women Authors

FOREWORD

Synclaire's first book of poetry is a testament to a young woman with great feelings who cares deeply for the people and causes that are dear to her heart. I feel blessed and honored to know her and to have had the opportunity to help mentor her these past two years. Synclaire has a uniquely deft hold on the English language and is an extremely versatile writer. Her poems are very personal reflections on life and her own emotional trials. She writes from the heart and is always willing and eager to share her poetry with others, even when they are of a very personal nature. A prolific writer, in my Creative Writing class, if I assigned one poem, Synclaire came to class the following day having written five – she is just that enthusiastic a writer. She often tells me that she prefers reading and writing to watching television or any other activity. I am very proud of Synclaire and of this wonderful book of poetry, which may be her first, but I guarantee, will not be her last. Synclaire is a rare gift on many levels, with an abundance of talent to share.

Congratulations on *Treading Water*, Synclaire!!

Chrys Cassetta

Synclaire was ten years old when I read her first poem. I remember asking her, "who wrote this" and seeing her expression of insult. The poetic writing was beyond her years, so I was impressed but not yet awake nor aware of the depth of my own daughter. Synclaire is an intellectual enigma who is often misunderstood as her external appearance directs most to draw simplistic conclusions of her silence. She is a hard core competitive athlete with an unwavering passionate voice for social injustice. However, her fight for the latter often turns inward and she writes to express her disdain. She tried to fit herself into a box and many she came in close contact with expected her to do the same. We all failed resulting in her feeling of failure. There is no fault as this is purely disconnection. Most clearly to me now is how hastily we draw conclusions and label people and situations we struggle to understand. And in doing so, we allow society to establish cosmetic answers to a complexity of life's challenges.

Synclaire wrote Treading Water when she was sixteen and seventeen years old with emotions that are visceral. Each poem lends a literary voice to her personal trials, to those who struggle in silence and to those in a fight for social justice. As I continue to read her poems, I experience deep pain and anguish for her pain and anguish and for my unawareness as a parent. I also feel incredible empowerment and pride. The countless lessons I have learned from my daughter are immeasurable and priceless. I am learning to be more perceptive, more insightful and most importantly, a better mother. My eyes are now wide open and I am filled up in the depth of my heart and my soul. I am truly learning who my beautiful soulful daughter is and I am excited for her life journey and to be a part of it. She continues to write and I am forever grateful.

Forever & Eternal Love,

Mom

Synclaire is a unique light to the world. As a baby, her smile was beautiful and would fuel me for an entire day. As she got older, her smiles became less frequent. I noticed how she began to analyze her surroundings and question her findings. Often times she would ask her mother and me for an explanation. Other times, she would draw conclusions from her own reading and research. I noticed Synclaire's methods of reasoning leaned towards social justice and equity.

Our family has travelled extensively throughout the world. My wife and I wanted our children to see and understand life in other states, countries, and even neighborhoods to help shape perspective. Synclaire's maturity and sense of purpose is evidence of the life she has lived combined with the innate spirit that is uniquely her own.

It is truly amazing to see my beautiful daughter continue to grow as she searches for her truth and strengthened as she journeys. I look forward to Synclaire's continued growth as a writer and as the woman she is becoming. Continue your journey, Precious!

I love you more than you can imagine.

Dad

DEDICATION

I thought painstakingly of just how dangerous the water inside my glass could be if I did not swim toward the life I most desired. I thought of the strength I felt when I swam through the waves; and I also thought to myself, despite the trials and tribulations of life, the anxiety filled waters were the only constant entity in my life.

So, I told myself I needed to embrace life and demand from it what I expected. While lost in my own thoughts, traveling the deeper regions of my own mind, I understood the liquid in my cup was the water of my own life. I saw clearly that there was nothing set in stone. My path in life will lead me exactly where I intend for it to take me. I knew that the more I wrote the more I would figure my life out, so I wrote and I write. I wrote every day for months until a collection of my thoughts were tangible idioms in my hands that I could offer to myself and the world around me.

The water in my glass has proven not to be just anxiety anymore. It is my tears and my sweat; it is my ink. The salt, grit and determination of my soul now surrounds and sullies the glass. But now my head is above water. I am no longer drowning. I am writing with my ink.

I am treading water.

DEAR YOU

For Colored Girls

"Being alive and being a woman is all I got, but being colored is a metaphysical dilemma I haven't conquered yet"

Born butterflies fetishized for the color of our wings
All that is majestic occurs in our internal chemistry
Atoms exploding into molecules
Bonding into melanin infused fireworks
They tried to steal our voice
Smashing it into glass containers
Confinement much like the chains of mahogany hipped women
On their way to a new world
That glass reflects our baby boys swinging from southern trees like rotten fruit
Waiting to be plucked and consumed by the fury of ignorance
The glass cuts like the feeling of having our hijab ripped from our heads
Our crown stolen,
Peering down to see the jewels of religion trembling from fear fueled hate
It cuts like plucking produce of the grounds from the sun rise until sunset
And having your payment equal to the price of a pack of bubblegum
That glass hides in the forged appreciation we are granted with
Telling us we are beautiful in spite of, not because of
But that same glass shines and shows what it truly means to be a colored girl
It is the braiding heritage in our scalps
It is the mixing secrets into the spice of nourishment
It is the blessing of our throats with the pride to speak our mother tongue
Our mother loves us
We came from her earth
She baptized us in protection
She sprinkled us with the heat into our pigment
Color is not a prison
It is a gift
Use it fiercely

Feminine

Girl emerging from womb
Blooming like flowers
To be plucked for her beauty
Expected to wilt when she is not
Soft sweet-scented skin
Cheeks rounded, full of grin
The first word to describe girl is "pretty"
Pretty diminishes any word said afterwards
Girl is now just "pretty nice", "pretty smart", "pretty amazing"
Girl is older with hips full and curves like coils
They are starting to notice her now
With body parts awakening, girl is in danger
Men drooling at the thought to be the first to enter her abyss
To traverse her ocean floor and swim in the water inside her
But once it has been taken girl is different
She is chewed up bubblegum ready to be spit out
Men wanting legs open
But expecting them to be closed
Girl is only supposed to open when she is told
Girl is forever a revolving door
Girl should not want things for herself
If she does tell you, tell her she is dirty
You tell her she is crude
When she does not respond to your advances you say she is rude
You think the worst day is when she was taught the word "no"
How dare she have the right to what was always yours?
"No", now has to be cut from her throat
It needs to be burned from her tongue to erase it's meaning
Girl is only measured on what she can give
She has been gathering for years, her hands are cramping
Feet tired and blistered from being hunted
Praying to one day to not be the prey
Girl never asked for it
Girl never asked for any of this shit
But how could anyone understand, when the stories have been past down for generations
That girl is just ripped bone
Made from and for men
Girl damned for wanting to taste knowledge when the flavor had been forbidden
Men praised for bleeding on battlefields

Girl shamed for bleeding from wombs
The naturalism of girl always needing concealment
The rawness of her meat needing to be cooked for men to feast upon
But girl was never built for you
Her hips will move mountains
Her eyes will start fires
Her lips will warn you of her storm
The majestic natural disaster that is girl
Your sisters need you as the danger bloats
With the patriarchy stepping on their throats

Womb and Heart

Mother
To raise your loves
Care without condition
Waves are crashing; no guide to help
Hold them.

Burnt Tastebuds

He placed candied promises on my tongue,
They turned to ash when he was done

Something I Always Forget

You are the most important person in your life

Jezebel

Wife of Ahab
Harlot
Meaning wicked one
Women today are still given her name
Placing the crowned title upon heads hoping that the sharp edges will pierce the scalp
Bleeding women
This is how we are seen
Bleeding from womb, bleeding from wound, bleeding from heart
We have been marked with bloody red "A" lettering
So the world could see our shame
"Adulator" they scream
Men collecting moonstones from the river, pebbles from streets, and boulders from the
Valley just to throw rocks at women criminalized for being raped
"Jezebel" they call her
"Jezebel", you ignore the name when it is not you being called
Tight skirts and low-cut dresses seem to tell them that we have no honor
Men listening to the so-called language of fabric saying, "yes"
As our throats are crying against it
"Jezebel", they call us again
"Nasty Woman"
Shame on us for taking our womanhood in our own hands
They tell us to remain giggling girls, submissive surrender
But they crave for the feminine fatale fascination
Bored with their wives
They crawl to the outskirts of the night for women to bring them their dreams
After they finished, they drop coins and again arises the sound of, "Jezebel"
Read of her again, listen closely
They took her love, heart torn from her chest
They took her children, soul stolen from womb
She was not thrown into the pit of dogs, she dove
Allowing the canine teeth to tear her apart just as the world did
There is no shame in Jezebel
The prophets wrote her as the demon
For they were burned for touching the power of her skin

Awaiting Land for The Celestial

Kumari Goddess is as if from another world
Feet never to touch the ground
A virgin girl bestowed with this honor
Pure, cool drinking water
The darkness never to grasp her
They know the dirtiness of the earth; they know how it can poison her
Funny how women of the night are described with the same phrase
"Feet never touching the ground"
The same ground where too many women are walked on
Footprints where their faces should be
The anticipation for the day that someone will enter you is a constant presence
Thinking about undressing, discovering, parts, but mostly the pain
It's not always physical
Waiting for them to call
Wondering if you were adequate
Wanting to feel something again
That pain transcends any broken skin
The soles of your feet never feeling the earth
Never allowing life between your toes
What purity is there in ignorance?"
An ocean is no less grand when someone swims in it
Virginity in nothing to be lost
Your body is not a set of keys
Nothing can be taken from you
All you have is to gain
I pray that you all walk one day wherever that terrain might be
And whatever it may look like.

Scissors

She was across the playground
The scent of bark
And the sweat on the monkey bars were pungent in the air
But you could only smell the bubble gum between her teeth

She was across the classroom
The lecture rattled on and on
And the constant tapping of impatient pencils pounded
But you could only hear her breath

She was at the party
The vodka infused juices stained your tongue
And the flavor of cheap beer filled you
But everything was washed clean when you tasted her lips on a dare

She was on the train
The broke down building peered into your eye line
And the graffiti held vibrancy
But it all dulled in comparison when you saw her eyelash kiss her cheek

She was at the grocery store
You were pursuing around the produce aisle, every peach feeling bruised
And the lettuce left a cool condensation on your surface
But then she grasped your hand and you realized what touch really was

There will be people telling you that you are just confused
That the puzzle of your mind is not complete without the feeling of manhood
They will show you how you are fetishized
A spectacle for hungry hypocritical eyes
That some people will only enjoy your love as long as it is a show for them

They will make you feel damned
That the Lord Himself will strike you down for wanting to hold her hand
Telling you that the nimbleness of her fingers
Are the very chains pulling you down to Hell

You will ask yourself if they are right
But they do not understand the legitimacy of it all
That a girl could have the ability to love and break you all in her hands
Just as much as any boy could

It's just you don't enjoy the feeling of their palms as much
Or maybe you are delighted in both hands
Loving someone is not a choice
But disrespecting someone is

There Is No Romance In Razor Blades

"How did you get those cuts?"
The question forms in their throats, it curls and rolls off their tongues in ease
The hesitation barely there, like your body is theirs to examine
You peer down at those marks
Banging your head for an answer to spew
The pot of excuses coming to a slow boil
"It was the cat"
"Box cutter, I got a package"
"I slipped"

Those scars seem to laugh at those lines, making this conversation a mockery
You look up again and see their eyes soften
Relaxed by the coating of your lies
The truth is too ugly

You think it looks too much like you
That is not true
They will ask you if those were done for attention
Like you wanted your pain to be broadcasted
They do not know what you are doing means
They cannot fathom what it gives you

There is nothing wrong with wanting your anguish to be spotlighted
There is nothing wrong with wanting to be seen
But this is not the way to do it
Everything around you has no control
You feel like the pain is what you want or you deserve it because it is yours

Clinging on to something that belongs to just you
But this isn't something for you to hold
I'm sorry if they laughed at you
I'm sorry if they threw curses at your name
I'm sorry if those heavy hands held you down

You are too soft for this sharp world
There is no weakness in you
But you cannot dissect yourself any longer
Cutting will not release anything, but your own power

There is no water in your veins to swim in
It is just blood
And it is not beautiful
Your wrists or hips are not flowers you need to cut free
They are just bone and tissue
And it is not romantic

There is nothing majestic about the emptiness in your chest
Your scarred skin will always be yours to war
It is not a trophy or shame
It is a map to direct you to places you will never return to,
And to areas you have yet to see.

The Weight of It All

O how her eyes filled with need
Chewed up lips that start to bleed
Her cracked bones forever cold
To hollow to even hold
A stomach craving to feed
A mind seeing this want as greed
The mirror starts to refer to another
Lungs that did not breathe, but only did smother
Her body was a magic trick
Slowly vanishing, making her sick
Her words of refusal never true, unfroze fingers turning blue
Her own physique ignited a mother's anger
Her the prey and hunger the hunter
She saw her looking meek and asked if she wanted to eat
Covered by her mystique
The girl smiled and said, "It's okay, I ate last week".
The people around her confused with guilt spinning
The girl wondered how she could keep thinning
Never knowing the grace that she holds
She tries to forget the future that is about to unfold
The bag of liquid dripping into her veins
Pretty petite bones was all she wanted to gain
She looks in the mirror and she cries
Thinking it is shame that she needs to hide
The world told her she was too much
The girl thought she was not enough
She was so much more that anyone could hold
Scared to be alone she fit into their mold
My darling girl, food is not the enemy
Starving can never be your remedy
I regret to tell you that there is still a war
You must fight every day to see what they have in store
You are winning because you are still here
Remember that you were and always will be beautiful, my dear.

The Brute Against The Tide

The violator is not a ghost
He is not an unearthly being that prowls the night and breaks into your chamber
He can be a smile
He could have even been a goodnight kiss
He is not always a he
The violator, a chameleon of society
Takes different forms
Embodying themselves as the meek sweet unassuming
We choke on their sheep's wool
Just to feel the wolf's bite
Bloody we emerge
Walking
Wining for the world to hear us
Mother Earth cries for her daughter
She aches for us
Her children succumbing to the dangerous terrain set out for them
How could the blame could be pinned upon us?
The nature of the act of bodily betrayal is too actual
The feeling of wood and vine trap us
Being held responsible for the entrapment
They blame us for our willingness to grin
Our freedom to parade in our own cloth
Our ability to walk along the pavement with the sun has forgotten our name
Our choice to consume beverages
We are blamed for our scent of womanhood
But nothing is your fault
Faulty lies within their hands
Fault lies between their legs
Fault lies on their godless tongue
Nothing of yours has been stolen
You are not an object
You are the only one able to claim yourself
You are free flowing water
An ocean everlasting
Let them choke on your salt
Never to swallow the flavor of you

Mistaking a Soulmate

You will meet this person one day
She will come in swiftly
Or he will enter abruptly
Or they will have been there all along
That person will hold you in places you marked as your tombstones
That person will not be able to fathom the contempt you have for those parts
That person will throw bibles at your softness
Never wanting to put the effort into an actual prayer
That person will treat you like
Braille
Never able to truly understand you without hands
Them always craving your warmth will feel like you forever need their palms
But you don't
She may have discovered the rhythm of your heart, but she also spilled your blood
He may have tasted your nectar, but he also fed you the
poison
They watched you flourish, but they also neglected to nourish you
That person will always be a love of yours
But they are not your only love
It was seasonal
They wanted you when the weather was warm and bright
The wind changed and you thought they did too
But that is not true
Their leaves just showed you the color of their intentions
Never forget the lessons he taught you
Remember the things she forgot or couldn't bring herself to give you
Whether that was loyalty, honesty or reciprocation
You are full without them
No person is here just for you
You can never ask someone of that
But you are here
You are enough
People will come and go
You are the only constant

Voices

Quiet,
Can you hear them?
The same words that called Joan
But this battle is not for France,
Darling.

Girls Who Wrote Words of Their Eulogy More Than Phone Numbers

We are born into a pink embrace
Looked at as sweet things
A treat to fulfill the worlds hunger
No one understands why "such pretty little girls" would fall in love with suicide
Suicide is not the bad boyfriend who forgets your calls
And peeps under other girl's skirts
Suicide is not the absentee father who remembers the color of his mistress's lipstick,
But not your birthday
Suicide is an old friend
Who will never let the hand of another strike you down
It always scares them how your cherry red nails could play with razors with ease
How your plush pink lips fit perfectly around a bottle
And how your porcelain skin seemed to crack the more they looked at it
But honey, suicide can never be your lover
It is a black widow
As soon as it enters you everything will parish
The bad will vanish, but so will the good
There is a secret that even your mother didn't tell you
You are allowed to want to die
You are allowed to "kill" parts of yourself
But, you are not allowed to kill all of you
Morn the smile that they once gave you
Morn the place between your thighs that was warm until their hands make you freeze
Morn each and every death of you
Plant flowers and visit the girl you once were
You can let the damp droplets dance out of your ducts
It is okay not to be that girl anymore
You are this woman now.

Some Boys Don't Know How to Swim

Said you were too much
He just craved a kiddy pool
Don't coax him with your seaweed
He lacks taste; can't handle salt.

The Worst Thing You Could Teach Your Daughter

"If he's mean to you that means he likes you"

This will make her question every intention of a male

This will cause her to excuse his actions

She will think that his thunderous storm will be the only way for her garden to grow

She will think that without his creation of rain that she will wilt

The flowers inside of you do not feed on tears

But he does, he demands to know that he's the only one that can damage your vines

He craves to be the single soul allowed to plant lilies in your cracked surface

There is nothing romantic about him comforting you for the pain that he caused.

Vixen

Lovers are nothing without her

Hips crashing waves and lips that cause faithful hands to stir

Eyes like knives as she turns marriage into murder

Produce

Brutally soft women

Tender as the fruit from branches and bushes

Their fingers leaving us bruised

But never tainting the taste

Our core was too raw

So they spit it out in fear

Ballad of the Burning Damsel

Sweet goddess of Spring
As she walked, the flowers began to sing
Born from nature's vessel, so pure
A demon saw and fell for her allure

Persephone was plucking peonies as he appeared
Thunder came with his presence and she was filled with fear
Dark chariot, four horses in stride
Young goddess had not time to hide

Hades deflowered and ripped her purity
Gone from her mother's bosom of security
She could hear the cries of souls
The demon's hands were always so cold

Demeter mourned for her daughter
Fury filled her, she did not allow the crops to water
That is how winter was born
The loss of Persephone left Demeter scorned

Persephone began to wilt
Hades grew in guilt
He fed her a seed from his pomegranate fruit
Persephone not aware it was corrupted by the root
As she digested, her soul was arrested
For Hades had trapped her, lost and unrequested

The deed had been done
The Underworld was hers to run
With Hell's fire by her side
Persephone was forced to be Hades' bride
Demeter knew that this was unjust
She had to rid her daughter of his clutch

Demeter could not have Persephone for eternity
This crushed Demeter's maternity
To release her daughter back into his arms for half the year
The action of this brought the world to tears

But the earth began to replenish under her hand
Demeter still felt the weight of Hades' command
That is why the earth's weather is divided
Because the different loves collided
There is warmth and growth
With the side of darkness, the world needed both

Maraschino Cherry

Bodies like scoops of ice cream
Pressed together
Sliding against one another
Mixing the flavors, letting tongues delight in the desire of dessert
The feeling of skin never chilled
Heat melting
Sticky
Different parts colliding, a taste so sweet
Sometimes it will just be bare pure cream
Other times decorated with toppings
To excite the flavor
Although there is nothing wrong with vanilla,
A hint of mint is always nice
Sometimes allowing the wafer to wrap around and take form
Meshing together soft and slow
Whipping the flavor furiously until it enriches your buds
Let every sprinkle shower you with sensation
During the first time the cherry might leak
Spilling red liquids all over the cream and maybe turning sour
Other times it will be so sweet you will forget to spit out the stem

Mediocre-Will

I forgot about everything
Except the way you said my name
That's a lie,
I'll always remember how you treated me
Like a donation
Taking all but the blame

The Ritual of Dawn

Arising in the early outskirts of dusk
Unleashing yourself from the sheets and cases
The warmth forgets you and the coolness remembers the curve of your waist
Peeling off the night's garments and stepping into the cold tiles to be cleansed
Water running along your skin
You turn up the heat to burn away the feeling
So you can forget who you are or what they made you become
Stepping out and steam rising from your pores
This is you
Pure and naked
Untainted by the poisons of your surroundings
Wrapping cotton around your parts, you venture back
Feeling the dampness between your toes
You look into the glass
The reflection returns your glance
The game begins
Each one demanding for dominance
The merry-go-round spins in your stomach
Colors colliding
Music playing
You are confused
Where did that girl go?
You imprint lilies on your hips
You apply pigment to your lips
Silk engorging flesh
They ask you why you take so long
They say you are perfect without it
But then when the facade fades and you walk around without paint
They ask you if you forgot slumber
Or if a virus has caught you
They want you born with golden eyelids and rouged cheekbones
To emerge for their liking and not to waste time
Break the hands of the clock

Walk barefoot and full
Dance pointed toe and bright
You are vibrant with or without decoration

Sincerely, Me

Bird

There is a canary in my heart that sings sweet songs
There is a canary in my heart that cries awful woes
This bird is never seen, it hides in my depth
He gnaws on my bones and begs to be released
Sometimes he tries to fly up through my throat
He desperately wants to be heard
I, however have always been a little off key
Never perfectly sound when it came to conversation
When I was younger I would bite boys who were mean to me
I would use my porcelain glass as protection from their taunts
Never to swallow the words that might poison my bird
My feelings have always been a ghost to me
A lingering shadow that can never be truly grasped
The canary sings ballads of love on nights where my skin feels the most cold
I too want the comfort of affection
To have someone else loosen the noose of contempt that I hang myself with
However, I could never bring myself to be that selfish
I would never ask someone to clip their wings just so I could fly
The canary longs for attachment
I have always shuddered from the touch of others
Not only to keep the blood off their hands, but for my own esteem
My adolescence was filled with broken things
I was always a pile of crushed bones
My canary would try to hum hymns of healing
My injuries just saw this as humorous
I am a dented body covered in scar tissue
My canary tries to conceal me with his feathers
He makes me a collage of paint and cloth
I wish that were enough to hide them
I was born during the time of melted snow and blooming flowers
I was told by my mother that the world seemed to sing on the day of my birth
But no song was louder than my bird
Through the years I've tried to hurt my canary

By drinking up potions, forgetting slumber and neglecting his nourishment
My canary's tune never to die
His rhymes have swept some of my darkest parts away
There are still days when the mirror and I disagree with the bird
His vision of a vibrant girl with elongated feathers is consumed by flames
Sometimes I choke on the ashes
My canary pushes past the dust and allows my lungs to breathe again
This bird bleeds more often than not
Sometimes I feel like I'm drowning in it
Gasping for the chance of dry land
Bird bleeds when he sees the tears of others
Bird bleeds when the beat of injustice is danced to
Bird bleeds when faces vanish
I fear for the day his wings are taken from me.

The U-Haul Hare

Boxes piled
Folded memories and broken thought
I forgot to smile
Dad got a new job; it's the same story, different plot
Mom's voice is loud
Brothers are throwing something, it found my head

Shoulders are slumped, affection I did not allow
But, Bun-Bun broke all the boundaries despite my impending dread
Cotton tail and fluffy ear drums my secrets to tell
He a blanket of security, a hand to hold
Coins leaving pockets with another house to sell
He let my rain pour, my emotions he would never try to mold

Forever listener, my quiet soldier
Fighting my battle, me soaking my blood in his fur
So ready to flee, he was lost and felt my skin getting colder
But wasn't he in my arms? He was so secure I was sure

I'm sorry Bun-Bun
My guilt is swollen
I cannot believe the shadows had won
Monsters from closets and bed swallowing, engulfing, never full

I'm sorry I left you
The grief never did dull
Heavy working hands must have dropped you
The delicacy of you never to resurface
You, you, you

Your silent words sung to me
A lullaby, I could never fall asleep
Sick of falling, I was constantly stumbling, drowning in sea
Bun-Bun I wish you were mine to keep

A child never forgets a friend
A girl bending and forced to break
A young woman did not want it to end
I miss you when the thunder comes and my hands ache
Wherever you may be I hope another found you

A little girl, a face new
An old man grasping your fur, letting his tired eyes rest in your softness
You were a crack in my darkened sky
Too pure for the likes of me.

Perfection in Glass

In my dreams
I saw my reflection

The monster was gone

Sharp teeth, smoothed out

Jagged nails; cut off

Chewed up skin spit out to a now smooth surface

Beautiful

But, above all you loved me

You loved me
You loved me.

Citrus

If I were to have a daughter I would name her Clementine
As soon as she enters this world I would dip her into the ocean
After months of swimming in my waters
I would want her to know that there is always something bigger
I would tell her to taste the salt that surrounds her
But never swallow it
She will know that not everything beautiful is hers to possess
I would braid secrets in her hair
That would whisper sweetnesses and shake her to her core
I would dress her in truth so the falsehoods of this world will always remain visible to her
I would kiss her hands everyday so she will never forget how to use them
I would send love letters to her throat so she will never allow hate to spew in her voice
I would tell her that she owns every word that emerges from her
To only apologize when the fault is her own
She will never be sorry for simply existing
She will know the grace in her foot prints
She will know the strength in her breath
I pray that one day someone will love her as much as I already do
To my darling, Clementine, I know how dark it all it is
Do not fear it
Just know that you are so much more.

The Inferno

The building is aflame
I can begin to feel my skin charcoal
Blackening and burning until it melts from my bones
I am glad to be rid of it
But how are my hands still cold?
The smoke danced in my lungs, swirling and curling until nothing more was left
I, nothing but ashes and bad timing
Finger nail marks covered the walls
How could I not feel the scratches?
I looked down
Torn fingers bleeding and crumbled but still cold
I am pacing
I can feel my words ready to leap from my tongue
But my teeth blocked their release
Where are you? I hear
Nothing is clear
Just grayed confusion
One of the walls fall
I am trapped
Broken ribs and buried lungs
My bones are caroling in rejoice
They were tired of the cries
Tears now dried up from my surface
Dehydrated and long
Where is she? I hear
The clocks have ran out
There is no time here
I have no time for it
But I had so much to do
The mere existence of me, now engorged by heat
Why are my hands still cold?
I rub them together to try to find a spark to ignite an ember within to combat the flames
Can she hear me? I hear
Synclaire? What is that?
I do not recognize it anymore
I am just abstract gibberish
Synclaire? There it is
I open my eyes
The flames are gone
There is no building

I am in the kitchen
My kitchen
She is there, my mother
And she's holding my hands
She begins to speak and it goes dark again.

Salted Woman

I've always known her
Her shadows always sleeping on my shoulders
Poking and prodding at my bones
She has hallowed me out
>This girl is so mean
>She is an angry bitch
>Fury fills her
>Drinking misery like wine
>She lets anguish ferment inside of her
>She sucks the salt from oceans
>Salt is the only reason why anything floats in the sea
>>She drops me into my watery grave as a gamble
>>She toys with the idea of how long my lungs will last
>>The water is cool
>>I am tangled in my own limbs like seaweed
>>The water trying to pull me apart
>>>I can see the creatures
>>>Searching the floor
>>>It's so dark
>>>My breath is no longer mine
>>>The water is trapped in my throat
>>>The tears muddled in the tide
>>>The sand scratches my skin
>>>Coating me with scars
>>>She's laughing at me
>>>>She rips at my skin
>>>>I turn and see the underwater treasure
>>>>It's been forgotten by its captors
>>>>I open it to see broken glass
>>>>It's much too clear
>>>>>I swim in its perfect clarity
>>>>>I see her through the glimmer
>>>>>And I realize that she is me

Scorpion's Poison

It all began with admiration
I stared in awe in familiarity of your features
You were like so many of the characters I created on the brightness of screens of my adolescence
No wonder why you referred to me as fawn
I was all legs and pupils staring at something
I wanted to be closer to
The flames from your scalp seemed to attract me
I was a pesky winged creature drawn to the light
Our signs were soulmates
I was so grateful when our waters had finally intertwined
And we swam in the pools together
Laughter catches my throat when my mind drifts off
To the idea of how easy it would be if our palms and lips could join in sincerity
How the cruelness of testosterone fueled selfishness
Would have never crept inside of our skin and burrowed into insecurity
I guess my lack of attraction to feminine softness is to blame
For our inability to ride into the sweet sorbet sunset
Our platonic affections are still a gleaming silver medal
You are my red cherry blossom girl
However, you decided to bloom in October
Which ironically is my favorite month
Ironic how we both bled the words " dear you" on to middle school journals
Ironic how we both secure our devices with the same four-digit code
Ironic how much I loved you
Ironic how you threw my name in the wind once my opinion did not mirror yours
Ironic how I thought you were the oxygen in my lungs
Ironic how you made me choke

Don't Be Mad

I'm sorry
I have taken all of your words
I would tear out my tongue, so you could have them back
I would leave it bleeding and raw just for you
I am the one your mother warned you about
Pretty pink girl with insides blue
Forgive me if I have ruined you
Please use my hair to lace up your wounds

Ocean

I sometimes forget that there are people like you

I often misplace the thought that I am not alone

I would like to thank each and every one of you for being here

I am grateful that you chose to keep breathing while the world was clenching your lungs

If tears have left your eyes while reading this

Remember that does not make you weak

Water is the beginning and end of everything

Just as you are

You cast out fires

And create monsoons

I hope you all recognize the strength in your tide

If the shadow of loneliness creeps on you, remember that you are surrounded in infinite waters

Waters that care deeply for your anguish

I send prayers to all of your homes

We are all here for a moment

And I am so glad I got to spend this moment with you.

About the Author

Synclaire Alexandria Warren is an enigma, a leader, an "old soul". In her authentic space, she is vibrant, funny, engaging and deeply compassionate and will light up any room she enters. Synclaire is passionate and an unwavering warrior in her fight for social justice. She is a rebel with a purpose.

Synclaire's exposure to philanthropy during her early childhood has fueled her desire to help others by participating in numerous charitable events and to spend time volunteering to read to children, feed the homeless, and collect clothing donations throughout the year. Extensive travel abroad with her family helped shape Synclaire's perspective and allowed for an easy transition for acceptance to serve as a Student Ambassador with People to People in France and England.

Synclaire's life experiences have contributed to her demonstrable compassion and empathy towards others and an insight beyond her years. Amidst her many social challenges during her high school journey, Synclaire has discovered her gift. She has an amazing ability to capture her thoughts and visceral emotions with the movement of her pen. She is a gifted creative writer capturing her life journey and those of her peers.

97018280R00028

Made in the USA
Columbia, SC
05 June 2018